The Next Generation Science Standards (NGSS) are reproduced with permission from the Department of Education.

By Jake Hunter, Beth Hunter and Bella Hunter.

The Diversity of Life: Soral's Bird Cafe

Student Edition

ISBN 978-1-952346-48-4

STEMTaught® **Grade 2**
Next Generation Science

2-LS4-1 Biological Evolution, Unity and Diversity:
Make observations of plants and animals to compare the diversity of life in different habitats.

Lesson Anchor
Make a bird feeder

There are so many different places where living things live! Let's observe some of the wonderful and diverse wildlife we can see right outside our classroom window. To attract wildlife, all you will need is your own bird feeder.

You can attract birds with a simple bird feeder.

What you'll need:

You can make a bird feeder out of just about anything. Reuse clean items from the trash to make your feeder. Find items such as these:

What you'll do:

Design and make a bird feeder at home or at school. You can use these designs to inspire your own creativity.

Tin Can Feeder

Cheerio Necklace Feeder

Milk Jug Feeder

Almond Butter Bread Heel Feeder

Almond Butter Toilet Paper Tube Feeder

Paper Milk Carton Feeder

This is my fantastic bird feeder thing-a-ma-jiggy!

I call it a ...

Draw your bird feeder here and show how it works.

Can you explain it?

 Think, Pair, Share!

What types of living things are found where you live?

Describe your habitat

No matter where you live, it is part of a habitat! You might live in a desert, near a forest, or on a mountain. Take a close look around to describe the habitat around you.

Describe the climate where you live. What is typical weather and rainfall like? What are normal temperatures across the seasons?

_____

_____

_____

Do you have any interesting land or water features nearby such as plains, hills, mountains, lakes, rivers or streams?

_____

_____

_____

What different types of plants and animals do you see where you live?

_____

_____

_____

_____

Soral's Bird Cafe

This is Soral. Soral loves birds. She wants to be an ornithologist when she grows up. An ornithologist is a bird scientist. Gophie is Soral's best friend. He likes birds too.

Decorate the cover of Soral's science journal.

Today Soral and Gophie are going to be scientists. Can you guess what they are going to do? Soral wants to see what birds are attracted to her birdseed. She makes a bird feeder and fills it with seeds. She calls it her bird cafe. She is going to participate in a feeder watch program!

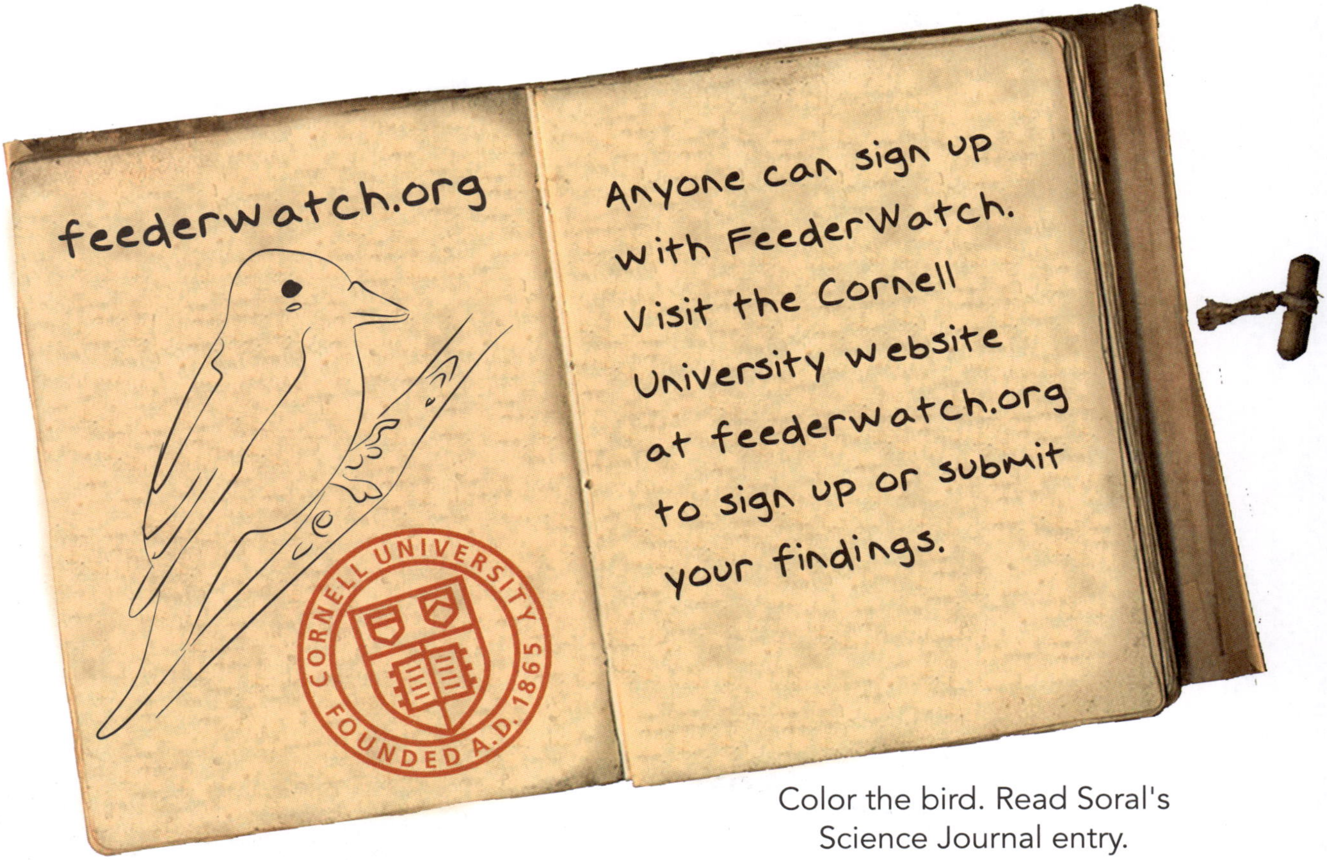
feederwatch.org
CORNELL UNIVERSITY FOUNDED A.D. 1865
Anyone can sign up with FeederWatch. Visit the Cornell University website at feederwatch.org to sign up or submit your findings.

Color the bird. Read Soral's Science Journal entry.

What types of birds live in your neighborhood? Can you describe them?

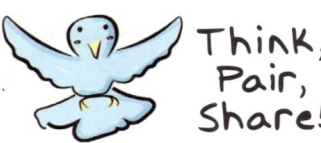

Think, Pair, Share!

Soral excitedly sets out all her seeds. Do you see any birds? Soral can't either. She will have to wait to see if birds can find her birdseed and her hummingbird feeder.

The next day Soral watches her feeder but she can't see any birds. Her Mom reminds her that experiments take time and patience. Maybe tomorrow the birds will come. Soral sadly records a "0" in her science journal because she did not see any birds at her feeder today.

Fill out Soral's observations for Day 1.

FeederWatch

How many birds do you see?

How many types of birds do you see?

Describe the birds that you see.

Why do you think there were not any birds at Soral's feeder today?

Think, Pair, Share!

It worked! The next morning Soral finds many small brown birds eating the corn from her feeder!

She runs to get her science journal. Help Soral by counting and recording the birds that she sees near the feeder. Write down the number in her journal.

Fill out Soral's observations for Day 2.

FeederWatch

HOW many birds do you see?

HOW many types of birds do you see?

Describe the birds that you see.

Why do you think there is only one type of bird at the feeder?

Think, Pair, Share!

The next day Gophie wants to help. He gets out his binoculars and climbs into the tree fort to quietly watch the birds. He pretends he is a pirate.

There are a lot of different birds today. Help Gophie and Soral with their observations.

Fill out Soral's observations for Day 3.

FeederWatch

How many birds do you see?

How many types of birds do you see?

Describe the birds that you see.

What makes each type of bird unique?

Think, Pair, Share!

Soral and Gophie have fun watching what birds come to their feeders. Today they spot some new visitors! Can you tell which birds are here for the first time?

Help Soral be a careful scientist by recording her feeder watch observations.

Fill out Soral's observations for Day 4.

FeederWatch

HOW many birds do you see?

HOW many types of birds do you see?

Describe the birds that you see.

Soral put nectar out to attract hummingbirds. Oh no! Mrs. Hummingbird is not happy! She is darting all around and flies away without taking a drink.

'What is wrong?' thought Soral as she stepped outside to take a closer look.

Ants! Quickly, Soral washes the ants off the feeder and moves it to another branch.

Soral has a lot to write about today. She learned that ants love sweet hummingbird nectar but hummingbirds do not like ants.

What type of food did Soral put out to attract hummingbirds?

How are the feeding habits of hummingbirds different than those of other birds?

 Think, Pair, Share!

Soral loves being a scientist. Thank you for helping her keep careful notes. Now Soral is going to make a graph. Graphing is fun, but don't eat the graphs, Gophie!

Make a graph to show how many birds visited Soral's bird feeders.

HOW many birds visited my feeder

| | Day 1 | Day 2 | Day 3 | Day 4 |

You can do this too!

You can be like Soral and watch for birds to come to your own feeder!

Birdwatching

Step 1: Make a bird feeder.

Step 2: Put birdseed or bread in your feeder.

Step 3: Check on your feeder later to see the birds.

Tweet?

Be an ornithologist!
Remember, a scientist that studies birds is called an ornithologist.

If you don't know what types of birds are visiting your feeder, that is okay! All you need to do is describe your birds.

Tip #1
Count all the birds both in the general area and around your feeders.

Use the bird foot and beak types on the next page to describe your birds.

You can be a scientist too! A birdwatching week is fun and easy to do. You can even share your data with Cornell University like Soral did.

Now Soral knows a lot more about the birds that live near her! And there is still so much to learn.

Observe the birds at your feeder

All birds have some things in common. For example, all birds have two wings, two feet, feathers and a beak. Different types of birds, however, have different traits that help them survive in their habitat. Although birds never have more than four toes, they have many different foot shapes.

Common Bird Foot Shapes

Feet for walking in mud

Three large toes in front help birds walk in mud and sand.

Feet for perching

Three toes in front and one in back help birds perch on branches.

Feet for climbing

Two toes in front and two in back help birds climb around.

Feet for Swimming

Webbed toes help birds swim or paddle through the water.

Birds beaks come in many shapes and sizes too! Different types of birds specialize in eating certain types of foods, and their beaks help them do it well. Birds can eat fish, seeds, insects and fruit. Some birds feed on nectar from flowers and others hunt smaller animals. Observe the birds at your feeder to identify what beak shapes they have.

Common Bird Beak Shapes

A beak for sipping nectar

A long, thin beak can reach deep into flowers to sip sweet nectar (hummingbirds, sunbirds).

A beak for catching insects

A short, thin beak is good for picking insects out of tight places and for collecting small seeds (songbirds).

A beak for cracking seeds

A short, strong beak is good for cracking the hard shells of seeds (many songbirds).

A beak for all purpose tasks

A large, strong beak is good for a bird that eats a variety of foods (crows and ravens).

A beak for skimming water

A wide bill is useful for skimming bits of food floating on the surface of water (ducks and swans).

Feeder observation log

Collect, record and organize your data. Count how many birds come to your feeder. Describe what they are doing.

Feeder Observation Day 1

Date _____   Number of birds _____

Describe the birds at your feeder. How many types are there? What do they look like? What are they doing?

_____

_____

_____

Feeder Observation Day 2

Date _____   Number of birds _____

Describe the birds at your feeder. How many types are there? What do they look like? What are they doing?

_____

_____

_____

Feeder Observation Day 3

Date _____ Number of birds _____

Describe the birds at your feeder. How many types are there? What do they look like? What are they doing?

_____

_____

_____

Feeder Observation Day 4

Date _____ Number of birds _____

Describe the birds at your feeder. How many types are there? What do they look like? What are they doing?

_____

_____

_____

Feeder Observation Day 5

Date _____ Number of birds _____

Describe the birds at your feeder. How many types are there? What do they look like? What are they doing?

_____

_____

_____

These are the birds at my feeder

Collect, record, and organize your data. Observe and describe how the birds at your feeder look.

Bird type 1

I observed a bird that looked like this ...

Draw and color the bird.

Circle the bird's foot and beak type.

Bird type 2

I observed a bird that looked like this ...

Draw and color the bird.

Circle the bird's foot and beak type.

Bird type 3

I observed a bird that looked like this ...

Draw and color the bird.

Circle the bird's foot and beak type.

Bird type 4

I observed a bird that looked like this ...

Draw and color the bird.

Circle the bird's foot and beak type.

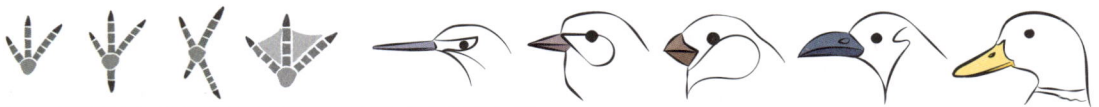

There are many types of living things

There are many different types of plants and animals. Some are furry, some have feathers, some have scales and others are slippery. Each of these creatures have special abilities that help them live well in their habitat. A habitat is the place where a living thing makes its home.

 Observe the photos of these habitats. Circle the photo that looks most like where you live.

Rainforest

Desert

Savanna

Alpine habitat

Temperate Forest

Tundra

How is your home most like the habitat photo you circled?

_____

_____

All living things are interconnected with their environment. In a habitat, living things depend on non-living things such as air, water, soil and sunlight.

The Parts of a Habitat

Circle the parts of a habitat that are non-living.

The Sun

Air

Soil

Water

Animals

Plants

Insects

Together, living and nonliving things in an area form a habitat.

The tropical rainforest of the Amazon

Rainforests get more rain than any other place on earth. Rainforests have more types of animal and plant life than any other habitat. More than half of all the world's species are found in rain forests. The trees in rainforests create almost half of the oxygen that we breathe. Rainforests are warm and get lots of moisture from rain.

Search Google Earth to explore the Amazon

Anori, Brazil

What is a rainforest habitat like?

Think, Pair, Share!

A rainforest can receive between 80 inches and 430 inches of rainfall per year.

To see how much rain falls in the Amazon try measuring out to 80 and 430 inches.

There are many different types of plants and animals that live in the rainforest.

Cut

The slow-moving sloth spends most of its life hanging upside down by its strong claws.

What do I eat?

The squirrel monkey moves quickly in trees. Its tail is used only for balance, not for climbing.

What do I eat?

Chameleons move slowly. They shoot out a long, sticky tongue to quickly catch their lunch.

What do I eat?

The green tree boa silently waits in trees for its lunch to come to it.

What do I eat?

The desert of Sonora, Arizona

Most **deserts** are hot and get very little rain. Some of the driest deserts, such as the Sahara, get as little as 10 centimeters (4 inches) per year. Try measuring 10 cm to see how much rain falls in the desert.

Cecropia tree leaves

Fruit and insects

Insects

Birds, bats & lizards

Use Google Earth to explore the the Sonoran desert.

Sonoran Desert National Monument

How are animals in the desert different from each other?

Think, Pair, Share!

There are many types of animals and plants that are well adapted to living with very little moisture in deserts.

Cut

The pygmy owl makes a safe home by digging a hole in a spiky saguaro cactus.

What do I eat?

The kangaroo rat gets water from the seeds and grass that it eats. It may never take a drink of water in its life.

What do I eat?

The rattlesnake is a predator that is most active at night when its food is awake.

What do I eat?

The desert iguana digs burrows in the sand to protect itself from the sun's heat during the daytime.

What do I eat?

The savanna grasslands

A **savanna** is a grassland with thin forests of trees. The forests of a savanna are thin enough that the trees do not block light from hitting the ground. The savanna is usually hot and dry, but it has a wet rainy season too.

Birds, insects & rodents

Mesquite and grass seed

Rodents and birds

Creosote bush leaves

Search Google Earth to explore a savanna.

Serengeti National Park, Tanzania

How are animals in the savanna different from each other?

Think, Pair, Share!

There are many types of animals and plants that are well adapted to living in the savanna.

Cut

The African elephant is the largest land mammal on earth. It eats about 200 pounds (90 kilograms) of food per day.

What do I eat?

The zebra constantly searches for water and food. They migrate 500 miles between the wet and dry seasons.

What do I eat?

Termites create mounds of dirt that they use for their protection. Inside the mound they grow their own food.

What do I eat?

The dung beetle shapes a piece of dung into a ball. It lays its eggs inside so its young can have food when they hatch.

What do I eat?

Alpine habitats

Alpine habitats are found all over the world in high mountains that are at least 10,000 feet above sea level. These habitats have a short growing season for plants in the summer. The elevation is too high for trees to grow.

Search Google Earth to explore an alpine habitat.

Mont Blanc, France

Grass and leaves

Fruit and insects

Fungus

Elephant dung

How are animals in an alpine habitat different from each other?

Think, Pair, Share!

There are many types of animals and plants that are well adapted to living in the cold alpine habitat.

Cut

A mountain goat's thick wool allows it to survive in temperatures as cold as -50° F (-45° C).

What do I eat?

Marmots hibernate, or sleep all winter to avoid the harsh conditions.

What do I eat?

Pika do not hibernate in winter. They make their dens under rocks and store grasses in their den.

What do I eat?

Tiny hairs all over the edelweiss plant and flowers protect it from harsh sunlight, drying out or freezing.

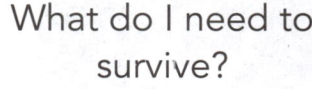
What do I need to survive?

41

Temperate forests

Temperate forests get a fair amount of rain and are warm in the summer and cold in the winter. The trees in a temperate forest are deciduous, meaning that they lose their leaves every year in winter.

Grass

Grass and insects

Plants

Fuzz

Search Google Earth to explore a temperate forest.

Olympic National Forest, Washington

Describe the animals from a forest habitat. What makes them unique?

Think, Pair, Share!

There are many types of animals and plants that are well adapted to living in temperate forests.

Cut

Bears eat lots of food to become fat in the summer. They hibernate in the winter when food is scarce.

Deer live in large groups called herds. They can run fast enough to outrun predators.

Raccoons are known for being very clever and can use their front paws like hands.

Squirrels are very good climbers. They live in trees and collect acorns and other seeds to eat.

43

Arctic tundra

The **arctic tundra** is a very cold habitat with harsh living conditions. The tundra is frozen most of the year and plants there look scrubby and small. Only the top few inches of soil thaw and the ground underneath remains frozen year round.

Berries, fish, insects

Grasses

Plants and animals

Seeds and nuts

Search Google Earth to explore an arctic tundra.

Northwest Territories, Canada

Describe the plants that you see in the Arctic tundra. What makes them unique?

Think, Pair, Share!

There are many types of animals and plants that are well adapted to living in the tundra.

Cut

Caribou have thick fur and strong legs that allow them to travel thousands of miles in search of food and water.

What do I eat?

The arctic fox has soft, thick white fur that help it blend into the snow so that it can't be seen while hunting.

What do I eat?

The arctic hare has white fur in the winter and brown fur in the summer so it can blend into its surroundings.

What do I eat?

Plants in the tundra are small because the soil lacks nutrients and roots can only penetrate a few inches into thawed soil.

What do I need to survive?

45

Polar ice habitats

At Earth's polar regions, the darkness of winter lasts for months and cold winds blow across the landscape. Even though its cold, polar regions have diverse wildlife above and below the ice.

Grasses

Small animals like voles

Plants, mosses & lichens

Sunlight and water

Search Google Earth to explore a polar ice habitat.

Northwest Territories, Canada

How are animals in the polar regions different from each other?

Think, Pair, Share!

There are many types of animals and plants that are well adapted to living in polar regions.

Cut

Polar bears are excellent swimmers and hunters. They roam the arctic ice in search of prey.

What do I eat?

The ringed seal has long claws on its front flippers used for digging breathing holes in the ice.

What do I eat?

The penguin is a bird that has wings that act as flippers. They can swim deep in the arctic waters in search of food.

What do I eat?

Orca whales are very smart and social. They hunt together in family groups and communicate with each other using sounds underwater.

What do I eat?

Seal

Squid, fish and shrimp

Fish

Fish, seal and penguin

Play the double dice habitat game

Each of Earth's habitats are very different from one another. Some are hot while others are cold. Some habitats are dry and other receive a lot of rainfall. To live in a habitat, plants and animals have many different unique qualities—like flippers, warm fur, sticky tongues and camouflage.

Play a game to show what you know about animals that live in Earth's habitats.

Prepare your paper cubes (dice):

1. Draw your habitats on the habitat cube.

2. Cut on the dotted lines.

3. Fold on the solid lines.

4. Fold tabs and tape to make both cubes.

How to play the game:

1. Roll both dice.

2. Read the name of the habitat on the first cube.

3. Read and follow the instructions on the second cube.

Prepare your habitat cube.

Habitats of the World

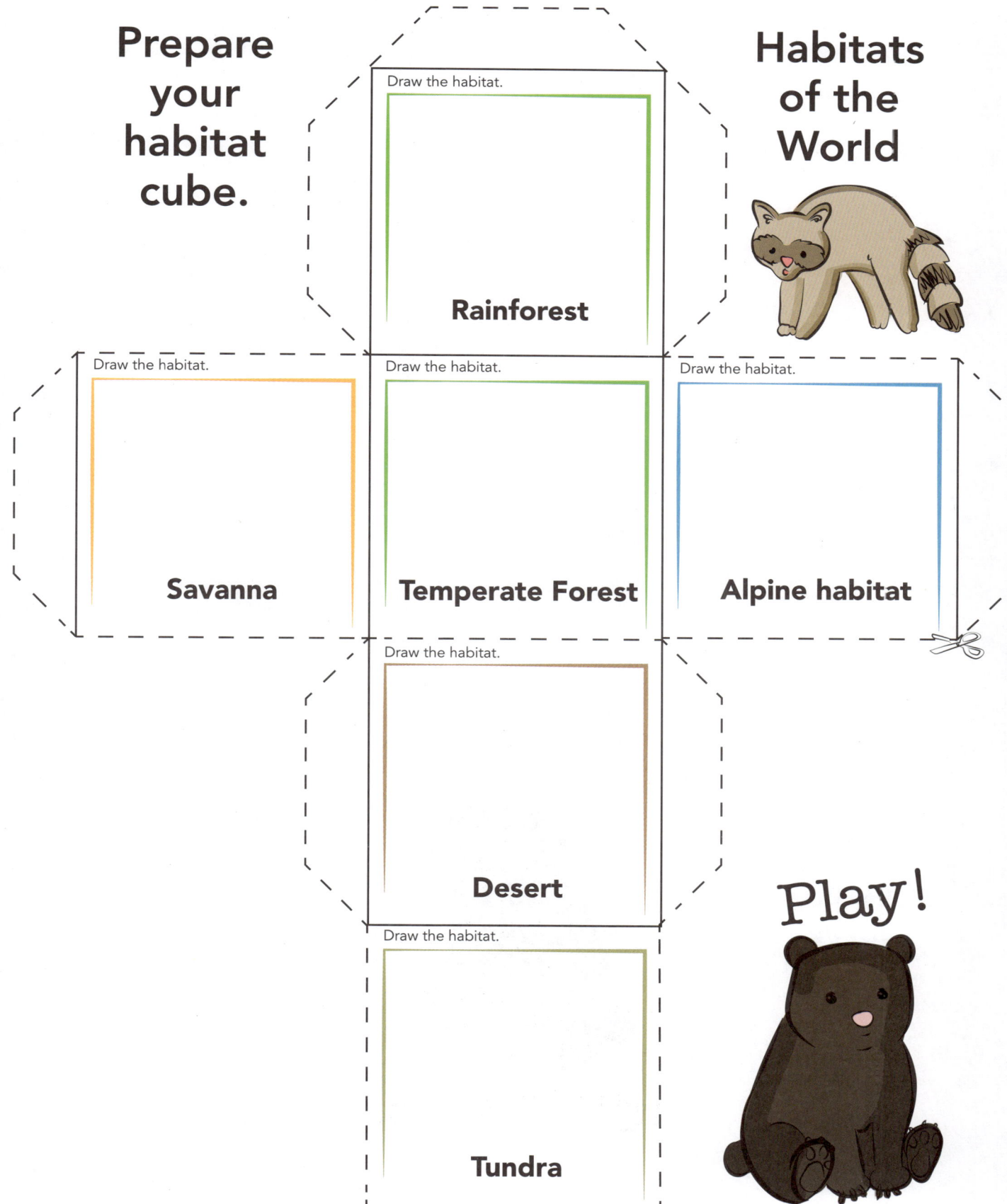

Draw the habitat.

Rainforest

Draw the habitat.

Savanna

Draw the habitat.

Temperate Forest

Draw the habitat.

Alpine habitat

Draw the habitat.

Desert

Draw the habitat.

Tundra

Play!

I ♡ STEM Tot®

Describe this habitat.

(temperature, rainfall, weather)

Prepare your question cube.

How are **animals** in this habitat **similar** to each other?

How are **animals** in this habitat **different** from one another?

What **animal abilities** are needed to survive in this habitat?

How are **plants** in this habitat **similar** to each other?

How are **plants** in this habitat **different** from each other?

Play!

I ♥ STEM Tot®

IT'S SONG TIME!

Get ready to sing a song about animal habitats! Sing these verses to the tune of **"Twinkle, Twinkle Little Star."**

Habitats of the World!

In the desert habitat

Lives a little kangaroo rat

In the day he takes a rest

In the night he leaves the nest

In the desert habitat

Lives a little kangaroo rat

A rainforest habitat

Is where the baby sloth lives at

Hanging in a tall, tall tree

Eating leaves, it moves slowly

A rainforest habitat

Is where the baby sloth lives at

In the dry savanna
Live a herd of zebra
They live upon a grassy plain
In one season they get some rain
In the dry savanna
Lives a little zebra

In the forest habitat
Is where the baby bear lives at
It eats all summer to grow strong
Then hibernates all winter long
In the forest habitat
Is where the baby bear lives at

A cold alpine habitat
Is where the mountain goat lives at
With wool to keep it very warm
It stays outside in winter storms
A cold alpine habitat
Is where the mountain goat lives at

The barren tundra habitat

Is where the caribou lives at

In search of food it runs for hours

It eats short grass and stubby flowers

The barren tundra habitat

Is where the caribou lives at

The icy polar habitat

Is where the little seal lives at

It pokes its head up through the ice

Its frozen home is very nice

The icy polar habitat

Is where the little seal lives at

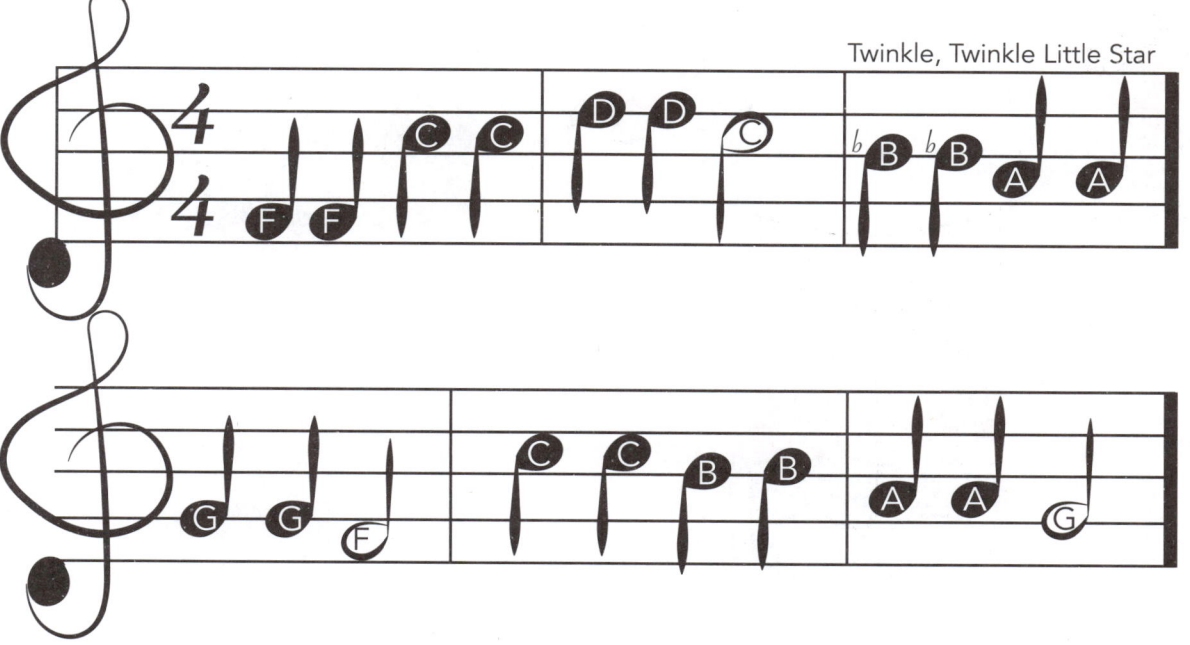

Twinkle, Twinkle Little Star

Living things are all around you

There are so many different animals and plants, and each of them has a special role to play in the environment.

Where do you find each of these living organisms? Are they up high? Down low? Or, are they by your toes?

Way up high

From the top of your shoulders to the sky

Down Low

From your ankles to the top of your shoulders

By my toes

Up to your ankles.

Cut out the organism cards and glue them into the spot where you would find them—up high, down low, or by your toes.

Cut

dandelions

tree

butterfly

roly poly

ant

hummingbird

weeds

spider

flower bush

clover

bird in flight

songbirds

ground squirrel

earthworm

bee

fly

Living organisms can be found everywhere—in the soil, under rocks, on the ground, in plants and trees, in water and even up in the sky.

Glue each plant and animal card where you think you would be most likely to find it.

What plant life and wildlife can you find?

Choose a special place at your school to look at all of the parts of your environment to see how diverse the plant life and wildlife is around you!

What you'll need:

- a pencil and your STEMTaught journal

What you'll do:

Go on a walk outside to observe the plants and animals that live way up high, down low and by your toes.

These students are observing plant and animal life on their school grounds.

You'll be surprised at how much life you find if you make close observations.

WAY UP HIGH (from your shoulders to the sky)

What I saw

How many?

_____   _____

_____   _____

_____   _____

_____   _____

DOWN LOW (from your ankles to the tops of your shoulders)

What I saw

How many?

_____   _____

_____   _____

_____   _____

_____   _____

_____   _____

BY MY TOES (up to your ankles)

What I saw

How many?

_____   _____

_____   _____

_____   _____

61

Fun-Dixie Journal Entry

What was your favorite part of this learning unit?
Draw and write about your experiences.

Royal
STEMTaught Post

When you read a great chapter in the STEMTaught Journal and do
the fun activities inside, sometimes you just want to write about it!

Fresh lava comes out of the Kilauea volcano in Hawaii.

Did the Hawaiian Islands form quickly or slowly?

It takes thousands of years for fresh volcanic rock to erode into soil that can support lush tropical forests.

45

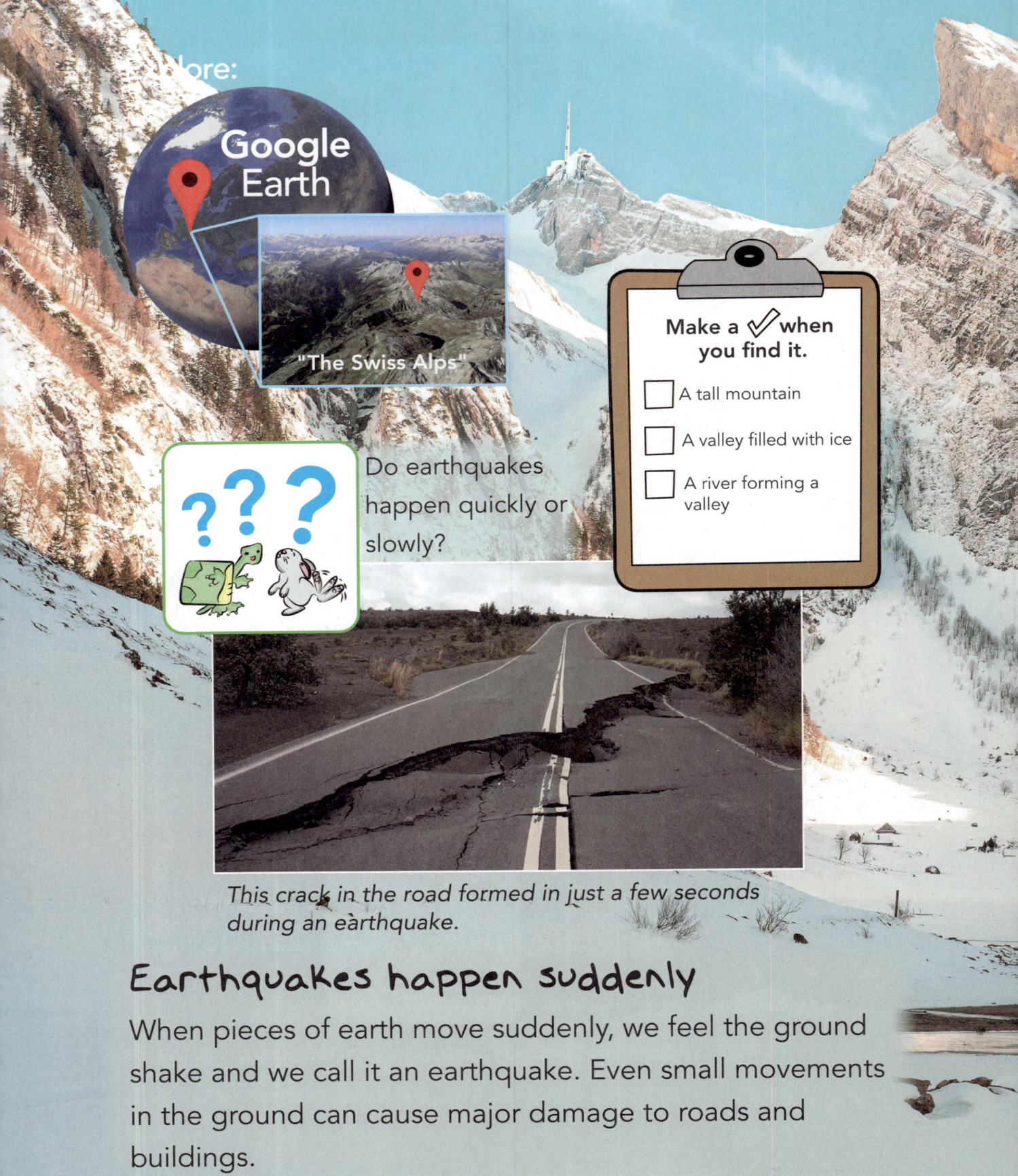

Explore:

Google Earth

"The Swiss Alps"

Make a ✓ when you find it.

☐ A tall mountain

☐ A valley filled with ice

☐ A river forming a valley

??? ?

Do earthquakes happen quickly or slowly?

This crack in the road formed in just a few seconds during an earthquake.

Earthquakes happen suddenly

When pieces of earth move suddenly, we feel the ground shake and we call it an earthquake. Even small movements in the ground can cause major damage to roads and buildings.

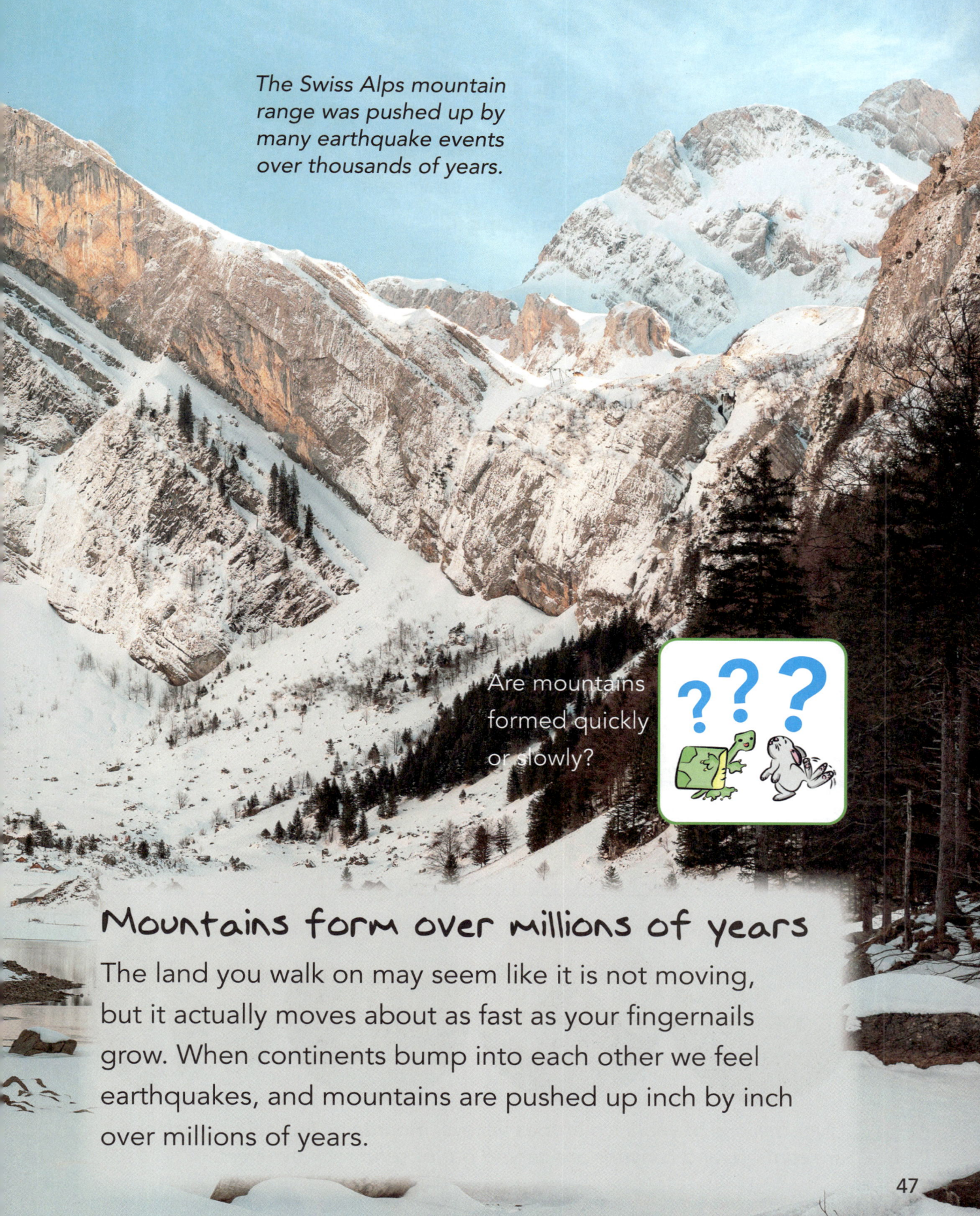

The Swiss Alps mountain range was pushed up by many earthquake events over thousands of years.

Are mountains formed quickly or slowly?

Mountains form over millions of years

The land you walk on may seem like it is not moving, but it actually moves about as fast as your fingernails grow. When continents bump into each other we feel earthquakes, and mountains are pushed up inch by inch over millions of years.

IT'S SONG TIME!

Get ready to sing about how the Earth can change both fast and slow! Sing these verses to the tune of **"Home on the Range."**

The Earth Changes Slow

Wherever I go, the earth changes slow

From the hills to the canyons below

The river's brisk flow, oh, it works to erode

And, shape all the landscapes I know

Slow, slow is the change

From the hills to the canyons below

The river's brisk flow, oh it works to erode

And, shape all the landscapes I know

Over millions of years ice erodes valleys, mountains are built up, islands are formed, and canyons are carved out of solid rock by rivers.

Now, sing a verse about how the Earth can change fast.

The Earth Changes Fast

Our Earth is so vast, it can change very fast

The Earth shakes, it erupts and it floods

The desert sands blow, moving dunes to and fro

A rock breaks, and it lands with a thud

Fast, fast is the change

The Earth shakes, it erupts and it floods

The desert sands blow, moving dunes to and fro

A rock breaks, and it lands with a thud

Which changes mentioned in each verse happen quickly and which happen slowly?

In just minutes, earthquakes can shake, floods rise up and volcanos erupt.
Dunes can change shape in a few weeks or months.

Erosion can cause problems for people

Erosion is a process that is always at work and it doesn't always take millions of years! Erosion can be very harmful to homes, farms and property. Strong rains can wash away the top layer of soil in a farmer's field. When this happens, crops don't grow as well.

Rainwater washed away fertile soil from this farmer's field leaving only rocks behind.

How can we protect a farm field from soil erosion?

Think, Pair, Share!

Leaving plants in a field after harvest can help protect the soil from being washed away between growing seasons. The roots of plants can help hold the soil together.

Ocean waves can wear away the shoreline. People must build homes far away from unstable coastlines so that they have safe spaces to live.

This house is at risk of falling into the ocean because ocean waves are eroding these sandy cliffs.

How can we protect property from coastal erosion?

Think, Pair, Share!

Sand piles up here...

... because rocks were put here.

The best way to protect a home from coastal erosion is to build far away from the water. People also build barriers using rocks to keep sand from washing away.

LIVING WITH WAVES
Improvised Engineering

The sounds of rushing water and rolling waves seem so pleasant and exciting, especially when we imagine a beautiful day full of surfing and sand castles. However, water is a mighty force! Crashing waves threaten houses in many places in the world including a world famous surf spot—Rocky Point, on the island of Oahu.

Compare the solutions to slow erosion at each beach house and decide which you think is best.

ROCKY POINT
LAT. 21-40.2 N   LONG. 158-02.7 W

Blue Sailor is a cute dog that loves going to Rocky Point. She knows how to hold her leash up as she runs really fast through the water and sand. She also likes to sniff for crabs.

Over the years, the waves have been pounding the coastline. Now, all the backyards are gone and everyone is worried that their homes could fall into the ocean next! Everyone is getting to work! Blue Sailor is investigating some of the latest neighborhood efforts to slow the erosion!

Help Blue Sailor analyze each of these different solutions for stopping erosion beneath the houses!

Strategy: A black tarp is stretched across the steep sandy slope.

Color the stars to show how good you think this idea is.

☆ ☆ ☆ ☆ ☆ (More stars means you like the idea better.)

How effective do you think this idea will be to slow erosion?

_____

_____

_____

THE STACKED SAND BAG HOUSE

My, that's a big, tall slope!

Engineering Closeup:

Sand bags →

Tarps covering stacks of sandbags

Strategy: Hundreds of sand bags are stacked and then covered with a big black tarp.

Color the stars to show how good you think this idea is.

(More stars means you like the idea better.)

How effective do you think this idea will be to slow erosion?

_____

_____

_____

_____

THE ROCK PILE HOUSE

Strategy: A big pile of rocks sits in front of the sandy slope to stop the wave action.

Color the stars to show how good you think this idea is.

☆ ☆ ☆ ☆ ☆ (More stars means you like the idea better.)

How effective do you think this idea will be to slow erosion?

_____

_____

_____

_____

THE CONCRETE WALL HOUSE

It looks like a castle to me!

Engineering Closeup:

Concrete

Telephone poles (wood)

Strategy: Poured cement and stacked telephone poles rest in front of the sandy slope.

Color the stars to show how good you think this idea is.

☆ ☆ ☆ ☆ ☆   (More stars means you like the idea better.)

How effective do you think this idea will be to slow erosion?

_____

_____

_____

_____

THE PURPLE PILLOW HOUSE

Engineering Closeup:

Purple pillow

Pillow cases filled with sand

I want the purple pillow!

Strategy: A pile of pillowcases filled with sand will catch the waves.

Color the stars to show how good you think this idea is.

☆ ☆ ☆ ☆ ☆ (More stars means you like the idea better.)

How effective do you think this idea will be to slow erosion?

_____

_____

_____

_____

THE TINY TRAILER HOUSE

Strategy: This house is on wheels and can be moved if needed.

Color the stars to show how good you think this idea is.

☆ ☆ ☆ ☆ ☆

(More stars means you like the idea better.)

How effective do you think this idea will be to slow erosion?

_____

_____

_____

_____

Compare and Analyze Solutions for Slowing Erosion

Because there is always more than one possible solution to a problem, it is useful to compare and test designs. Try modeling each house's design solution. Use materials such as cloth to represent a tarp, a piece of wood to represent a cement wall and small rocks to represent boulders or sand bags. Put sand in a small container, build your solution to slow erosion and slosh water to mimic the waves.

Why are people trying to prevent erosion and what will make them successful?

_____

_____

_____

Which solution do you think is best? Why do you think so?

_____

_____

_____

Which solution do you think is the worst? Why do you think so?

_____

_____

_____